Thug Journal

www.gratitudeandmore.ca

This journal is for the disgruntled individual—you know who you are. You need to write shit down but don't need a fluffy journal to get shit done. Well, look no further. This journal is for you.

If you are offended by foul language—put this book down immediately! I'm not even kidding. Put it down now.

If you are still reading, then this journal is for you. Use it however the fuck you want.

Each day has two pages; there is one lined page for any free writing and one page with daily prompts. There is also a Weekly Check-In page that allows you to review the previous week—use or don't use it, I don't really give a shit.

Enjoy your Thug Life over the next nine weeks.

For more information on the wide variety of journals we offer, visit us at www.gratitudeandmore.ca

Leah

Date:	Disgruntled Scale (1-10):

I am not angry about (a.k.a. grateful for):

Was I sarcastic today? (Of course you were....how sarcastic were you?):

Total number of WTF's:	Number of fucks given:
Did I get some exercise today?	Do I care?

I need to work on:

How well did I practice restraint?	My plan for tomorrow:
How many people did I offend today?	

When I want your opinion, I'll give it to you.

Date:	Disgruntled Scale (1-10):

I am not angry about (a.k.a. grateful for):

Was I sarcastic today? (Of course you were....how sarcastic were you?):

Total number of WTF's:	Number of fucks given:
Did I get some exercise today?	Do I care?

I need to work on:

How well did I practice restraint?	My plan for tomorrow:
How many people did I offend today?	

_____

_____

_____

_____

_____

_____

_____

_____

_____

_____

_____

_____

_____

_____

_____

_____

_____

_____

_____

_____

I'm not sarcastic—you're stupid.

Date:	Disgruntled Scale (1-10):
I am not angry about (a.k.a. grateful for):	
Was I sarcastic today? (Of course you were....how sarcastic were you?):	
Total number of WTF's:	Number of fucks given:
Did I get some exercise today?	Do I care?
I need to work on:	
How well did I practice restraint?	My plan for tomorrow:
How many people did I offend today?	

_____

_____

_____

_____

_____

_____

_____

_____

_____

_____

_____

_____

_____

_____

_____

_____

_____

_____

_____

_____

_____

Oh, you're offended? You should hear my inside voice.

Date:	Disgruntled Scale (1-10):

I am not angry about (a.k.a. grateful for):

Was I sarcastic today? (Of course you were....how sarcastic were you?):

Total number of WTF's:	Number of fucks given:
Did I get some exercise today?	Do I care?

I need to work on:

How well did I practice restraint?	My plan for tomorrow:
How many people did I offend today?	

Just fuck off. There is no try.

Date:	Disgruntled Scale (1-10):

I am not angry about (a.k.a. grateful for):

Was I sarcastic today? (Of course you were....how sarcastic were you?):

Total number of WTF's:	Number of fucks given:
Did I get some exercise today?	Do I care?

I need to work on:

How well did I practice restraint?	My plan for tomorrow:
How many people did I offend today?	

_____

_____

_____

_____

_____

_____

_____

_____

_____

_____

_____

_____

_____

_____

_____

_____

_____

_____

_____

_____

_____

_____

OMG—Do you know who I am?!

Date:	Disgruntled Scale (1-10):

I am not angry about (a.k.a. grateful for):

Was I sarcastic today? (Of course you were....how sarcastic were you?):

Total number of WTF's:	Number of fucks given:
Did I get some exercise today?	Do I care?

I need to work on:

How well did I practice restraint?	My plan for tomorrow:
How many people did I offend today?	

Get in line—I'll blame you in a minute.

Date:	Disgruntled Scale (1-10):

I am not angry about (a.k.a. grateful for):

Was I sarcastic today? (Of course you were....how sarcastic were you?):

Total number of WTF's:	Number of fucks given:

Did I get some exercise today?	Do I care?

I need to work on:

How well did I practice restraint?	My plan for tomorrow:
How many people did I offend today?	

Are you fucking kidding me? It's still not Friday?!

<u>Additional Notes:</u>

WEEKLY CHECK-IN

Did I harm anyone? *(Thinking about punching someone in the face doesn't count)*	Was it intentional?

Did I get to remove useless people from my life?

Have I been a good friend to the thugs around me?	Do I need to help someone who gives less fucks than I do?

Do I have an emotional blockage? A hardening of the attitudes?

Why don't I have...

Why do I always get...

Am I suffering from Envy of Friends Who Have Shit I Want?

Date:	Disgruntled Scale (1-10):

I am not angry about (a.k.a. grateful for):

Was I sarcastic today? (Of course you were....how sarcastic were you?):

Total number of WTF's:	Number of fucks given:
Did I get some exercise today?	Do I care?

I need to work on:

How well did I practice restraint?	My plan for tomorrow:
How many people did I offend today?	

_____

_____

_____

_____

_____

_____

_____

_____

_____

_____

_____

_____

_____

_____

_____

_____

_____

_____

_____

_____

The more people I meet the more I realize I fucking hate people.

Date:	Disgruntled Scale (1-10):

I am not angry about (a.k.a. grateful for):	

Was I sarcastic today? (Of course you were....how sarcastic were you?):	

Total number of WTF's:	Number of fucks given:
Did I get some exercise today?	Do I care?

I need to work on:	

How well did I practice restraint?	My plan for tomorrow:
How many people did I offend today?	

How are you doing? Just kidding, I don't really give a shit.

Date:	Disgruntled Scale (1-10):

I am not angry about (a.k.a. grateful for):

Was I sarcastic today? (Of course you were....how sarcastic were you?):

Total number of WTF's:	Number of fucks given:
Did I get some exercise today?	Do I care?

I need to work on:

How well did I practice restraint?	My plan for tomorrow:
How many people did I offend today?	

LOL, TTYL, TTFN. Really? GFYMF.

Date:	Disgruntled Scale (1-10):

I am not angry about (a.k.a. grateful for):

Was I sarcastic today? (Of course you were....how sarcastic were you?):

Total number of WTF's:	Number of fucks given:
Did I get some exercise today?	Do I care?

I need to work on:

How well did I practice restraint?	My plan for tomorrow:
How many people did I offend today?	

I just watched Hoarders...my place is a goddamn palace.

Date:	Disgruntled Scale (1-10):

I am not angry about (a.k.a. grateful for):

Was I sarcastic today? (Of course you were....how sarcastic were you?):

Total number of WTF's:	Number of fucks given:

Did I get some exercise today?	Do I care?

I need to work on:

How well did I practice restraint?	My plan for tomorrow:
How many people did I offend today?	

_____

_____

_____

_____

_____

_____

_____

_____

_____

_____

_____

_____

_____

_____

_____

_____

_____

_____

_____

_____

No really, I still don't give a shit.

Date:	Disgruntled Scale (1-10):

I am not angry about (a.k.a. grateful for):

Was I sarcastic today? (Of course you were....how sarcastic were you?):

Total number of WTF's:	Number of fucks given:
Did I get some exercise today?	Do I care?

I need to work on:

How well did I practice restraint?	My plan for tomorrow:
How many people did I offend today?	

Sigh. I have no more fucks to give.

Date:	Disgruntled Scale (1-10):
I am not angry about (a.k.a. grateful for):	
Was I sarcastic today? (Of course you were....how sarcastic were you?):	
Total number of WTF's:	Number of fucks given:
Did I get some exercise today?	Do I care?
I need to work on:	
How well did I practice restraint?	My plan for tomorrow:
How many people did I offend today?	

I do speak sarcasm, but there is no translation for stupidity.

Additional Notes:

WEEKLY CHECK-IN

Did I harm anyone? *(Did they deserve it?)*	Was it intentional?

Did I get to remove useless people from my life?	

Have I been a good friend to the thugs around me?	Do I need to help someone who gives less fucks than I do?

Do I have an emotional blockage? A hardening of the attitudes?

Why don't I have...

Why do I always get...

Am I suffering from Envy of Friends Who Have Shit I Want?

Date:	Disgruntled Scale (1-10):

I am not angry about (a.k.a. grateful for):	

Was I sarcastic today? (Of course you were....how sarcastic were you?):	

Total number of WTF's:	Number of fucks given:
Did I get some exercise today?	Do I care?

I need to work on:	

How well did I practice restraint?	My plan for tomorrow:
How many people did I offend today?	

_____

_____

_____

_____

_____

_____

_____

_____

_____

_____

_____

_____

_____

_____

_____

_____

_____

_____

_____

_____

You spend much time with cows...'cause all I hear is bullshit.

Date:	Disgruntled Scale (1-10):
I am not angry about (a.k.a. grateful for):	
Was I sarcastic today? (Of course you were....how sarcastic were you?):	
Total number of WTF's:	Number of fucks given:
Did I get some exercise today?	Do I care?
I need to work on:	
How well did I practice restraint?	My plan for tomorrow:
How many people did I offend today?	

My superpower is not working because you are still here.

Date:	Disgruntled Scale (1-10):
I am not angry about (a.k.a. grateful for):	
Was I sarcastic today? (Of course you were....how sarcastic were you?):	
Total number of WTF's:	Number of fucks given:
Did I get some exercise today?	Do I care?
I need to work on:	
How well did I practice restraint?	My plan for tomorrow:
How many people did I offend today?	

_____

_____

_____

_____

_____

_____

_____

_____

_____

_____

_____

_____

_____

_____

_____

_____

_____

_____

I wish you understood that when I give you a high five, I'm imagining
that they are all middle fingers.

Date:	Disgruntled Scale (1-10):

I am not angry about (a.k.a. grateful for):

Was I sarcastic today? (Of course you were....how sarcastic were you?):

Total number of WTF's:	Number of fucks given:

Did I get some exercise today?	Do I care?

I need to work on:

How well did I practice restraint?	My plan for tomorrow:
How many people did I offend today?	

_____

_____

_____

_____

_____

_____

_____

_____

_____

_____

_____

_____

_____

_____

_____

_____

_____

_____

_____

**I stopped coffee, swearing and judging people—I'm just kidding.
You'd be dead if I did that.**

Date:	Disgruntled Scale (1-10):

I am not angry about (a.k.a. grateful for):

Was I sarcastic today? (Of course you were....how sarcastic were you?):

Total number of WTF's:	Number of fucks given:
Did I get some exercise today?	Do I care?

I need to work on:

How well did I practice restraint?	My plan for tomorrow:
How many people did I offend today?	

_____

_____

_____

_____

_____

_____

_____

_____

_____

_____

_____

_____

_____

_____

_____

_____

_____

_____

_____

No, I do not play well with others. How do you not know this?

Date:	Disgruntled Scale (1-10):
I am not angry about (a.k.a. grateful for):	
Was I sarcastic today? (Of course you were....how sarcastic were you?):	
Total number of WTF's:	Number of fucks given:
Did I get some exercise today?	Do I care?
I need to work on:	
How well did I practice restraint?	My plan for tomorrow:
How many people did I offend today?	

Drink all the wine you want, but if you touch my coffee I'll fucking kill you.

Date:	Disgruntled Scale (1-10):

I am not angry about (a.k.a. grateful for):

Was I sarcastic today? (Of course you were....how sarcastic were you?):

Total number of WTF's:	Number of fucks given:

Did I get some exercise today?	Do I care?

I need to work on:

How well did I practice restraint?	My plan for tomorrow:
How many people did I offend today?	

_____

_____

_____

_____

_____

_____

_____

_____

_____

_____

_____

_____

_____

_____

_____

_____

_____

_____

_____

_____

_____

_____

I'm going to close my eyes and count to ten and if you're still here....
then you're really fucking stupid.

Additional Notes:

WEEKLY CHECK-IN

Did I harm anyone?	Was it intentional?

Did I get to remove useless people from my life?

Have I been a good friend to the thugs around me?	Do I need to help someone who gives less fucks than I do?

Do I have an emotional blockage? A hardening of the attitudes?

Why don't I have...

Why do I always get...

Am I suffering from Envy of Friends Who Have Shit I Want?

Date:	Disgruntled Scale (1-10):

I am not angry about (a.k.a. grateful for):

Was I sarcastic today? (Of course you were....how sarcastic were you?):

Total number of WTF's:	Number of fucks given:

Did I get some exercise today?	Do I care?

I need to work on:

How well did I practice restraint?	My plan for tomorrow:
How many people did I offend today?	

_____

_____

_____

_____

_____

_____

_____

_____

_____

_____

_____

_____

_____

_____

_____

_____

_____

_____

_____

I'd go out, but I have an entire season to binge on….and I don't like you.

Date:	Disgruntled Scale (1-10):

I am not angry about (a.k.a. grateful for):

Was I sarcastic today? (Of course you were....how sarcastic were you?):

Total number of WTF's:	Number of fucks given:
Did I get some exercise today?	Do I care?

I need to work on:

How well did I practice restraint?	My plan for tomorrow:
How many people did I offend today?	

_____

_____

_____

_____

_____

_____

_____

_____

_____

_____

_____

_____

_____

_____

_____

_____

_____

_____

**What did we do before Google? We wasted a lot of fucking time,
that's what we did.**

Date:	Disgruntled Scale (1-10):

I am not angry about (a.k.a. grateful for):

Was I sarcastic today? (Of course you were....how sarcastic were you?):

Total number of WTF's:	Number of fucks given:
Did I get some exercise today?	Do I care?

I need to work on:

How well did I practice restraint?	My plan for tomorrow:
How many people did I offend today?	

_____

_____

_____

_____

_____

_____

_____

_____

_____

_____

_____

_____

_____

_____

_____

_____

_____

_____

_____

You need to practice more yoga so you can get your head out of your ass.

Date:	Disgruntled Scale (1-10):

I am not angry about (a.k.a. grateful for):

Was I sarcastic today? (Of course you were....how sarcastic were you?):

Total number of WTF's:	Number of fucks given:
Did I get some exercise today?	Do I care?

I need to work on:

How well did I practice restraint?	My plan for tomorrow:
How many people did I offend today?	

_____

_____

_____

_____

_____

_____

_____

_____

_____

_____

_____

_____

_____

_____

_____

_____

_____

_____

_____

Uckfay off, eh? I love Pig Latin Canadians.

Date:	Disgruntled Scale (1-10):

I am not angry about (a.k.a. grateful for):

Was I sarcastic today? (Of course you were....how sarcastic were you?):

Total number of WTF's:	Number of fucks given:
Did I get some exercise today?	Do I care?

I need to work on:

How well did I practice restraint?	My plan for tomorrow:
How many people did I offend today?	

_____

_____

_____

_____

_____

_____

_____

_____

_____

_____

_____

_____

_____

_____

_____

_____

_____

_____

_____

_____

My mom told me...just kidding. My family doesn't speak to me.

Date:	Disgruntled Scale (1-10):

I am not angry about (a.k.a. grateful for):

Was I sarcastic today? (Of course you were....how sarcastic were you?):

Total number of WTF's:	Number of fucks given:
Did I get some exercise today?	Do I care?

I need to work on:

How well did I practice restraint?	My plan for tomorrow:
How many people did I offend today?	

You may think it's about you, but really, it's all about me.

Date:	Disgruntled Scale (1-10):

I am not angry about (a.k.a. grateful for):

Was I sarcastic today? (Of course you were....how sarcastic were you?):

Total number of WTF's:	Number of fucks given:
Did I get some exercise today?	Do I care?

I need to work on:

How well did I practice restraint?	My plan for tomorrow:
How many people did I offend today?	

_____

_____

_____

_____

_____

_____

_____

_____

_____

_____

_____

_____

_____

_____

_____

_____

_____

_____

_____

_____

_____

_____

Coffee: Because being a grumpy fucktard in the morning is frowned upon.

Additional Notes:

WEEKLY CHECK-IN

Did I harm anyone? *(Thinking about punching someone in the face doesn't count)*	Was it intentional?

Did I get to remove useless people from my life?

Have I been a good friend to the thugs around me?	Do I need to help someone who gives less fucks than I do?

Do I have an emotional blockage? A hardening of the attitudes?

Why don't I have...

Why do I always get...

Am I suffering from Envy of Friends Who Have Shit I Want?

Date:	Disgruntled Scale (1-10):

I am not angry about (a.k.a. grateful for):

Was I sarcastic today? (Of course you were....how sarcastic were you?):

Total number of WTF's:	Number of fucks given:

Did I get some exercise today?	Do I care?

I need to work on:

How well did I practice restraint?	My plan for tomorrow:
How many people did I offend today?	

I'd offer to help, but I just don't like you.

Date:	Disgruntled Scale (1-10):

I am not angry about (a.k.a. grateful for):

Was I sarcastic today? (Of course you were....how sarcastic were you?):

Total number of WTF's:	Number of fucks given:
Did I get some exercise today?	Do I care?

I need to work on:

How well did I practice restraint?	My plan for tomorrow:
How many people did I offend today?	

_____

_____

_____

_____

_____

_____

_____

_____

_____

_____

_____

_____

_____

_____

_____

_____

_____

_____

_____

_____

_____

Have you always been an annoying little fuck?

Date:	Disgruntled Scale (1-10):

I am not angry about (a.k.a. grateful for):

Was I sarcastic today? (Of course you were....how sarcastic were you?):

Total number of WTF's:	Number of fucks given:

Did I get some exercise today?	Do I care?

I need to work on:

How well did I practice restraint?	My plan for tomorrow:
How many people did I offend today?	

No, I'm not busy; I just don't want to be seen with you.

Date:	Disgruntled Scale (1-10):
I am not angry about (a.k.a. grateful for):	
Was I sarcastic today? (Of course you were....how sarcastic were you?):	
Total number of WTF's:	Number of fucks given:
Did I get some exercise today?	Do I care?
I need to work on:	
How well did I practice restraint?	My plan for tomorrow:
How many people did I offend today?	

_____

_____

_____

_____

_____

_____

_____

_____

_____

_____

_____

_____

_____

_____

_____

_____

_____

_____

_____

_____

Are you a professional fucker-upper?

Date:	Disgruntled Scale (1-10):

I am not angry about (a.k.a. grateful for):

Was I sarcastic today? (Of course you were....how sarcastic were you?):

Total number of WTF's:	Number of fucks given:
Did I get some exercise today?	Do I care?

I need to work on:

How well did I practice restraint?	My plan for tomorrow:
How many people did I offend today?	

_____

_____

_____

_____

_____

_____

_____

_____

_____

_____

_____

_____

_____

_____

_____

_____

_____

_____

_____

_____

If you don't like my Plan A, you're going to fucking hate my Plan B.

Date:	Disgruntled Scale (1-10):

I am not angry about (a.k.a. grateful for):

Was I sarcastic today? (Of course you were....how sarcastic were you?):

Total number of WTF's:	Number of fucks given:

Did I get some exercise today?	Do I care?

I need to work on:

How well did I practice restraint?	My plan for tomorrow:
How many people did I offend today?	

_____

_____

_____

_____

_____

_____

_____

_____

_____

_____

_____

_____

_____

_____

_____

_____

_____

_____

_____

Five minutes ago...before you opened your mouth?
I would like those minutes back please.

Date:	Disgruntled Scale (1-10):

I am not angry about (a.k.a. grateful for):

Was I sarcastic today? (Of course you were....how sarcastic were you?):

Total number of WTF's:	Number of fucks given:
Did I get some exercise today?	Do I care?

I need to work on:

How well did I practice restraint?	My plan for tomorrow:
How many people did I offend today?	

I'm suffering from SWF: Stupid Work Fucktards.

<u>Additional Notes:</u>

WEEKLY CHECK-IN	
Did I harm anyone? *(Did they deserve it?)*	Was it intentional?
Did I get to remove useless people from my life?	
Have I been a good friend to the thugs around me?	Do I need to help someone who gives less fucks than I do?
Do I have an emotional blockage? A hardening of the attitudes?	
Why don't I have...	
Why do I always get...	
Am I suffering from Envy of Friends Who Have Shit I Want?	

Date:	Disgruntled Scale (1-10):

I am not angry about (a.k.a. grateful for):

Was I sarcastic today? (Of course you were....how sarcastic were you?):

Total number of WTF's:	Number of fucks given:
Did I get some exercise today?	Do I care?

I need to work on:

How well did I practice restraint?	My plan for tomorrow:
How many people did I offend today?	

Too bad your ancestors didn't have tickets on the Titanic.

Date:	Disgruntled Scale (1-10):

I am not angry about (a.k.a. grateful for):

Was I sarcastic today? (Of course you were....how sarcastic were you?):

Total number of WTF's:	Number of fucks given:
Did I get some exercise today?	Do I care?

I need to work on:

How well did I practice restraint?	My plan for tomorrow:
How many people did I offend today?	

_____

_____

_____

_____

_____

_____

_____

_____

_____

_____

_____

_____

_____

_____

_____

_____

_____

_____

_____

_____

_____

_____

_____

_____

Let's play Hide 'N Fuck Off.

Date:	Disgruntled Scale (1-10):

I am not angry about (a.k.a. grateful for):

Was I sarcastic today? (Of course you were....how sarcastic were you?):

Total number of WTF's:	Number of fucks given:
Did I get some exercise today?	Do I care?

I need to work on:

How well did I practice restraint?	My plan for tomorrow:
How many people did I offend today?	

You don't like my language? That's okay, I don't like anything about you.

Date:	Disgruntled Scale (1-10):

I am not angry about (a.k.a. grateful for):

Was I sarcastic today? (Of course you were....how sarcastic were you?):

Total number of WTF's:	Number of fucks given:
Did I get some exercise today?	Do I care?

I need to work on:

How well did I practice restraint?	My plan for tomorrow:
How many people did I offend today?	

Coffee, sugar and WTF's get me through the day.

Date:	Disgruntled Scale (1-10):
I am not angry about (a.k.a. grateful for):	
Was I sarcastic today? (Of course you were....how sarcastic were you?):	
Total number of WTF's:	Number of fucks given:
Did I get some exercise today?	Do I care?
I need to work on:	
How well did I practice restraint?	My plan for tomorrow:
How many people did I offend today?	

I can go from zero to bat-shit crazy in 2.6 seconds. I'm talented that way.

Date:	Disgruntled Scale (1-10):

I am not angry about (a.k.a. grateful for):

Was I sarcastic today? (Of course you were....how sarcastic were you?):

Total number of WTF's:	Number of fucks given:
Did I get some exercise today?	Do I care?

I need to work on:

How well did I practice restraint?	My plan for tomorrow:
How many people did I offend today?	

I'm made of blood, sweat and boatloads of profanity.

Date:	Disgruntled Scale (1-10):

I am not angry about (a.k.a. grateful for):

Was I sarcastic today? (Of course you were....how sarcastic were you?):

Total number of WTF's:	Number of fucks given:
Did I get some exercise today?	Do I care?

I need to work on:

How well did I practice restraint?	My plan for tomorrow:
How many people did I offend today?	

Did you actually graduate or did your teachers just feel sorry for you?

Additional Notes:

WEEKLY CHECK-IN

Did I harm anyone?	Was it intentional?

Did I get to remove useless people from my life?

Have I been a good friend to the thugs around me?	Do I need to help someone who gives less fucks than I do?

Do I have an emotional blockage? A hardening of the attitudes?

Why don't I have...

Why do I always get...

Am I suffering from Envy of Friends Who Have Shit I Want?

Date:	Disgruntled Scale (1-10):

I am not angry about (a.k.a. grateful for):

Was I sarcastic today? (Of course you were....how sarcastic were you?):

Total number of WTF's:	Number of fucks given:
Did I get some exercise today?	Do I care?

I need to work on:

How well did I practice restraint?	My plan for tomorrow:
How many people did I offend today?	

Am I a fucking genius or are you...never mind, I'm a fucking genius.

Date:	Disgruntled Scale (1-10):

I am not angry about (a.k.a. grateful for):

Was I sarcastic today? (Of course you were....how sarcastic were you?):

Total number of WTF's:	Number of fucks given:
Did I get some exercise today?	Do I care?

I need to work on:

How well did I practice restraint?	My plan for tomorrow:
How many people did I offend today?	

I don't talk to assholes, it makes me feel like shit.

Date:	Disgruntled Scale (1-10):
I am not angry about (a.k.a. grateful for):	
Was I sarcastic today? (Of course you were....how sarcastic were you?):	
Total number of WTF's:	Number of fucks given:
Did I get some exercise today?	Do I care?
I need to work on:	
How well did I practice restraint?	My plan for tomorrow:
How many people did I offend today?	

_____

_____

_____

_____

_____

_____

_____

_____

_____

_____

_____

_____

_____

_____

_____

_____

_____

_____

_____

"There" is no better than "Here" unless You go over There
while I stay here.

Date:	Disgruntled Scale (1-10):

I am not angry about (a.k.a. grateful for):

Was I sarcastic today? (Of course you were....how sarcastic were you?):

Total number of WTF's:	Number of fucks given:
Did I get some exercise today?	Do I care?

I need to work on:

How well did I practice restraint?	My plan for tomorrow:
How many people did I offend today?	

_____

_____

_____

_____

_____

_____

_____

_____

_____

_____

_____

_____

_____

_____

_____

_____

_____

_____

_____

_____

_____

_____

Please fuck the fuck off. Thank you. (Sorry, I'm Canadian)

Date:	Disgruntled Scale (1-10):

I am not angry about (a.k.a. grateful for):

Was I sarcastic today? (Of course you were....how sarcastic were you?):

Total number of WTF's:	Number of fucks given:
Did I get some exercise today?	Do I care?

I need to work on:

How well did I practice restraint?	My plan for tomorrow:
How many people did I offend today?	

_____

_____

_____

_____

_____

_____

_____

_____

_____

_____

_____

_____

_____

_____

_____

_____

_____

_____

_____

_____

We don't have family gatherings, we have hostage taking events.

Date:	Disgruntled Scale (1-10):

I am not angry about (a.k.a. grateful for):

Was I sarcastic today? (Of course you were....how sarcastic were you?):

Total number of WTF's:	Number of fucks given:
Did I get some exercise today?	Do I care?

I need to work on:

How well did I practice restraint?	My plan for tomorrow:
How many people did I offend today?	

I only do family vacations if my family can't come.

Date:	Disgruntled Scale (1-10):

I am not angry about (a.k.a. grateful for):

Was I sarcastic today? (Of course you were....how sarcastic were you?):

Total number of WTF's:	Number of fucks given:

Did I get some exercise today?	Do I care?

I need to work on:

How well did I practice restraint?	My plan for tomorrow:
How many people did I offend today?	

_____

_____

_____

_____

_____

_____

_____

_____

_____

_____

_____

_____

_____

_____

_____

_____

_____

_____

I'm grateful for my family, they make me look
more brilliant every damn day.

Additional Notes:

WEEKLY CHECK-IN	
Did I harm anyone? *(Thinking about punching someone in the face doesn't count)*	Was it intentional?
Did I get to remove useless people from my life?	
Have I been a good friend to the thugs around me?	Do I need to help someone who gives less fucks than I do?
Do I have an emotional blockage? A hardening of the attitudes?	
Why don't I have...	
Why do I always get...	
Am I suffering from Envy of Friends Who Have Shit I Want?	

Date:	Disgruntled Scale (1-10):

I am not angry about (a.k.a. grateful for):

Was I sarcastic today? (Of course you were....how sarcastic were you?):

Total number of WTF's:	Number of fucks given:
Did I get some exercise today?	Do I care?

I need to work on:

How well did I practice restraint?	My plan for tomorrow:
How many people did I offend today?	

I don't need therapy—I need you to leave me the fuck alone.

Date:	Disgruntled Scale (1-10):

I am not angry about (a.k.a. grateful for):

Was I sarcastic today? (Of course you were....how sarcastic were you?):

Total number of WTF's:	Number of fucks given:

Did I get some exercise today?	Do I care?

I need to work on:

How well did I practice restraint?	My plan for tomorrow:
How many people did I offend today?	

_____

_____

_____

_____

_____

_____

_____

_____

_____

_____

_____

_____

_____

_____

_____

_____

_____

_____

Is it wrong that I look forward to the silent treatment from my family?

Date:	Disgruntled Scale (1-10):
I am not angry about (a.k.a. grateful for):	
Was I sarcastic today? (Of course you were....how sarcastic were you?):	
Total number of WTF's:	Number of fucks given:
Did I get some exercise today?	Do I care?
I need to work on:	
How well did I practice restraint?	My plan for tomorrow:
How many people did I offend today?	

Our family doesn't put the fun in dysfunction;
we put the alcohol in alcoholic.

Date:	Disgruntled Scale (1-10):

I am not angry about (a.k.a. grateful for):

Was I sarcastic today? (Of course you were....how sarcastic were you?):

Total number of WTF's:	Number of fucks given:
Did I get some exercise today?	Do I care?

I need to work on:

How well did I practice restraint?	My plan for tomorrow:
How many people did I offend today?	

If your outsides matched your insides, you'd just be one big piece of shit.

Date:	Disgruntled Scale (1-10):

I am not angry about (a.k.a. grateful for):

Was I sarcastic today? (Of course you were....how sarcastic were you?):

Total number of WTF's:	Number of fucks given:
Did I get some exercise today?	Do I care?

I need to work on:

How well did I practice restraint?	My plan for tomorrow:
How many people did I offend today?	

_____

_____

_____

_____

_____

_____

_____

_____

_____

_____

_____

_____

_____

_____

_____

_____

_____

_____

_____

_____

_____

My goal today is to just not kill anyone.

Date:	Disgruntled Scale (1-10):

I am not angry about (a.k.a. grateful for):

Was I sarcastic today? (Of course you were....how sarcastic were you?):

Total number of WTF's:	Number of fucks given:
Did I get some exercise today?	Do I care?

I need to work on:

How well did I practice restraint?	My plan for tomorrow:
How many people did I offend today?	

I don't have resting bitch face, I have I don't give a fuck face.

Date:	Disgruntled Scale (1-10):

I am not angry about (a.k.a. grateful for):

Was I sarcastic today? (Of course you were....how sarcastic were you?):

Total number of WTF's:	Number of fucks given:
Did I get some exercise today?	Do I care?

I need to work on:

How well did I practice restraint?	My plan for tomorrow:
How many people did I offend today?	

My mind is like a dangerous neighbourhood.
Sometimes even I enter at my own risk.

Additional Notes:

WEEKLY CHECK-IN	
Did I harm anyone? *(Did they deserve it?)*	Was it intentional?
Did I get to remove useless people from my life?	
Have I been a good friend to the thugs around me?	Do I need to help someone who gives less fucks than I do?
Do I have an emotional blockage? A hardening of the attitudes?	
Why don't I have...	
Why do I always get...	
Am I suffering from Envy of Friends Who Have Shit I Want?	

Date:	Disgruntled Scale (1-10):

I am not angry about (a.k.a. grateful for):

Was I sarcastic today? (Of course you were....how sarcastic were you?):

Total number of WTF's:	Number of fucks given:

Did I get some exercise today?	Do I care?

I need to work on:

How well did I practice restraint?	My plan for tomorrow:
How many people did I offend today?	

_____

_____

_____

_____

_____

_____

_____

_____

_____

_____

_____

_____

_____

_____

_____

_____

_____

_____

**Fuck this shit. I'm simply not capable of being an adult today.
And tomorrow isn't looking good either.**

Date:	Disgruntled Scale (1-10):

I am not angry about (a.k.a. grateful for):

Was I sarcastic today? (Of course you were....how sarcastic were you?):

Total number of WTF's:	Number of fucks given:
Did I get some exercise today?	Do I care?

I need to work on:

How well did I practice restraint?	My plan for tomorrow:
How many people did I offend today?	

You should be very worried when I'm quiet. That's usually when I'm
planning my revenge.

Date:	Disgruntled Scale (1-10):

I am not angry about (a.k.a. grateful for):	

Was I sarcastic today? (Of course you were....how sarcastic were you?):	

Total number of WTF's:	Number of fucks given:
Did I get some exercise today?	Do I care?

I need to work on:	

How well did I practice restraint?	My plan for tomorrow:
How many people did I offend today?	

You have no idea of the restraint I am practicing right now.
I'm actually kicking the shit out of you in my head.

Date:	Disgruntled Scale (1-10):

I am not angry about (a.k.a. grateful for):

Was I sarcastic today? (Of course you were....how sarcastic were you?):

Total number of WTF's:	Number of fucks given:
Did I get some exercise today?	Do I care?

I need to work on:

How well did I practice restraint?	My plan for tomorrow:
How many people did I offend today?	

It's not me, it's you. It's definitely all you.

Date:	Disgruntled Scale (1-10):

I am not angry about (a.k.a. grateful for):

Was I sarcastic today? (Of course you were....how sarcastic were you?):

Total number of WTF's:	Number of fucks given:
Did I get some exercise today?	Do I care?

I need to work on:

How well did I practice restraint?	My plan for tomorrow:
How many people did I offend today?	

I'm grateful for coffee, chocolate and the fact that no one can
read my mind.

Date:	Disgruntled Scale (1-10):

I am not angry about (a.k.a. grateful for):

Was I sarcastic today? (Of course you were....how sarcastic were you?):

Total number of WTF's:	Number of fucks given:
Did I get some exercise today?	Do I care?

I need to work on:

How well did I practice restraint?	My plan for tomorrow:
How many people did I offend today?	

The first step on the road to recovery is admitting you're a fucktard.

Date:	Disgruntled Scale (1-10):

I am not angry about (a.k.a. grateful for):

Was I sarcastic today? (Of course you were....how sarcastic were you?):

Total number of WTF's:	Number of fucks given:

Did I get some exercise today?	Do I care?

I need to work on:

How well did I practice restraint?	My plan for tomorrow:
How many people did I offend today?	

If you don't like my sarcastic comments, stop saying stupid things.

<u>Additional Notes:</u>

WEEKLY CHECK-IN

Did I harm anyone?	Was it intentional?

Did I get to remove useless people from my life?

Have I been a good friend to the thugs around me?	Do I need to help someone who gives less fucks than I do?

Do I have an emotional blockage? A hardening of the attitudes?

Why don't I have...

Why do I always get...

Am I suffering from Envy of Friends Who Have Shit I Want?

People Worth Contacting

Contact Information:

Name: _____

Phone #: _____

e-mail: _____

Address: _____

_____

Birthday: _____

Met: _____

Name: _____

Phone #: _____

e-mail: _____

Address: _____

_____

Birthday: _____

Met: _____

Contact Information:

Name: _____

Phone #: _____

e-mail: _____

Address: _____

_____

Birthday: _____

Met: _____

Name: _____

Phone #: _____

e-mail: _____

Address: _____

_____

Birthday: _____

Met: _____

Contact Information:

Name: _____

Phone #: _____

e-mail: _____

Address: _____

_____

Birthday: _____

Met: _____

Name: _____

Phone #: _____

e-mail: _____

Address: _____

_____

Birthday: _____

Met: _____

Contact Information:

Name: _____

Phone #: _____

e-mail: _____

Address: _____

_____

Birthday: _____

Met: _____

Name: _____

Phone #: _____

e-mail: _____

Address: _____

_____

Birthday: _____

Met: _____

Contact Information:

Name: _____

Phone #: _____

e-mail: _____

Address: _____

_____

Birthday: _____

Met: _____

Name: _____

Phone #: _____

e-mail: _____

Address: _____

_____

Birthday: _____

Met: _____

Contact Information:

Name: _____

Phone #: _____

e-mail: _____

Address: _____

_____

Birthday: _____

Met: _____

Name: _____

Phone #: _____

e-mail: _____

Address: _____

_____

Birthday: _____

Met: _____